THE POWER OF
LEADERSHIP

by
John C. Maxwell

RIVER
OAK
PUBLISHING

The Power of Leadership
ISBN 1-58919-411-X
Copyright © 2001 by John C. Maxwell

Published by RiverOak Publishing
P.O. Box 700143
Tulsa, Oklahoma 74170-0143

Introduction

Powerful leaders are readers! Even those who don't read widely read wisely. They often clip articles and quotes to file for future use, which has been a practice of mine for more than thirty years.

Over the years, I have often been asked to share my quote collection. *The Power of Leadership* is my fulfillment of those requests for material on leadership. Long ago, I learned that if you want to quote like a leader, you must *note* like a leader. In this book, you will find great material to help you build your leadership power. So be ready to take some notes and file some quotes!

—John C. Maxwell

Leadership is influence.

—John C. Maxwell

This is my favorite definition of leadership. It's a simple, straightforward, one-word description that places leadership within everyone's reach. All of us can exercise a certain degree of influence on someone, at some point, in some place. Leadership isn't about titles, positions, or flowcharts. It's about one life influencing another.

Character is power.

—Booker T. Washington

The first lesson we must each learn is that broad leadership is built from deep character. An infrastructure of great character is essential to support great conduct. The trust and involvement of our followers will be parallel to the level of our own character.

Use power to help people.
For we are given power not to
advance our own purposes, nor
to make a great show in the world,
nor a name. There is but one just use
of power, and it is to serve people.

—George Bush

THE POWER OF
LEADERSHIP

George Bush was right. We abuse our power when we utilize it for self-gain. One of the buzzwords of the '90s was the word "empower." It simply means to give your power away. This is what people are longing for their leaders to do. This truth is echoed by Jesus in Matthew 20:26: "... whoever wishes to become great among you shall be your servant."

Failure can be divided into those who thought and never did and into those who did and never thought.

—Reverend W.A. Nance

Someone once told me that the world has two kinds of people: thinkers and doers. They then said, "the thinkers need to do more, and the doers need to think more." I have always tried to do both—reflect and act. When I have combined the two, I have greatly reduced the odds of failure.

Leaders must be close
enough to relate to others,
but far enough ahead
to motivate them.

—John C. Maxwell

I have always believed this principle. It beautifully combines the necessity of both relationship and vision. I must live with the people to understand them and earn their trust. However, I am only their "buddy" if that's all I do. To be a leader, I must live with God and move with Him beyond where the people are. If they are to follow me, I must be ahead of them.

Leadership is the capacity
to translate vision into reality.

—Warren G. Bennis

Most of us learn the hard way that
leadership is not merely having a vision.
Anyone can dream. Effective leadership is
knowing how to lay down the action steps
for yourself and the organization so that the
vision can be realized. This requires us to be
practical and to understand the process along
the way.

You manage things; you lead people.

—Grace Murray Hopper
Admiral, U.S. Navy (Retired)

I must have articulated this principle a hundred times during my years as a pastor. People don't want to be managed, organized, stereotyped, tagged, or filed. That's what you do with things in an office. People are dynamic and must be led through love and relationship.

A man must be
big enough to admit his mistakes,
smart enough to profit from them,
and strong enough to correct them.

One of the least talked about prerequisites for leadership is a strong sense of personal security. Without it, I sabotage myself and my organization. With it, I can handle mistakes with perspective, and have the ability to admit them, profit from them and correct them.

I don't know the key to success,
but the key to failure is
trying to please everybody.

—Bill Cosby

One of the weaknesses of many of
today's leaders is our compulsion to take
surveys. It happens in politics, and it happens
in churches. A leader must go beyond being
a people-pleaser to being a God-pleaser. If
our need for the people's affirmation
exceeds our need for God's affirmation,
we're in trouble. Leadership sometimes
means doing what's unpopular.

You are the same today that
you are going to be five years
from now except for two things:
the people with whom you associate
and the books you read.

—Charles "Tremendous" Jones

I read this statement by Charlie Jones years ago, and I've become more convinced of its truth as time goes by. If we plan to become great, we must determine to expose ourselves to great books and great people. Their input will influence our growth more than anything else. Choose both wisely.

No matter what size the bottle,
the cream always came to the top.

—Charles Wilson
President, GE

Pastoring in the Midwest, I quickly learned that people are somewhat like fresh milk from a cow. At first glance it all looks the same. But eventually the cream rises to the top. Similarly you'll find that given time, the "movers and shakers" naturally rise to the top. Simply watch and wait.

A ship in a harbor is safe, but
that is not what ships were built for.

We've all seen this statement on a plaque or poster somewhere. What a great reminder it is that safety, security, and survival are not meaningful goals for our lives. If we're going to get anywhere, we're going to have to risk venturing into the unknown. Life is about adventure, not maintenance.

You can have brilliant ideas,
but if you can't get them across,
your ideas won't get you anywhere.

—Lee Iacocca

I discovered this truth as I observed my
staff attempting to cast a vision to the
people in their departments. Ideas alone can't
harness a group of people. We can only
move to accomplish a goal when the vision
is cast clearly, creatively, and consistently.

THE POWER OF
LEADERSHIP

Asking "Who ought to be the boss?"
is like asking "Who ought to be the
tenor in the quartet?" Obviously,
the man who can sing tenor.

—Henry Ford

I love the simple, unpretentious logic of
Henry Ford. He cuts through the red tape of
human politics, suggesting that leadership
isn't a matter of tenure or title, but ability.
The appropriate question is, "Who can get
the job done?"

Nothing great was ever achieved
without enthusiasm.

—Ralph Waldo Emerson

I am an attitude nut. I just happen to believe that an enthusiastic attitude places a leader above his peers, opens his mind to creativity, and provides motivation to his people. "Enthusiasm" is taken from two root words: "en" and "theos," meaning "God within." If we have God living on the inside of us, we ought to be enthusiastic!

The best executive is the one
who has sense enough to pick good
men to do what he wants done, and
self-restraint enough to keep from
meddling with them while they do it.

— Theodore Roosevelt

I have always tried to lead my staff this way: I select and salary my team based upon ability and productivity. When I place a leader in a position that fits his/her abilities, it is apparent in the overall quality of their work. That done, I leave them to reach the goals we've set in whatever way they choose. I don't care so much how they get to the goal, as long as they reach it!

The single most important factor
in determining the climate of an
organization is the top executive.

—Charles Galloway

Everything rises and falls on leadership. Once a leader has been directing an organization (or church) for two years or more, the personality, atmosphere, and problems of that organization are a result of his leadership. When you see him, you see the organization.

You must live with people to
know their problems, and live
with God in order to solve them.

—P.T. Forsyth

This truism combines two very
important ingredients for a leader. A leader is
called to stand in the gap between the
people and God. We must be close enough
to the people to represent them (their needs
and struggles) before God. At the same time,
we must be close enough to God to
represent Him (His answers and direction)
before the people. This is the key balancing
act before us.

Reportedly, IBM's Tom Watson was asked if he was going to fire an employee who made a mistake that cost IBM $600,000. He said, "No, I just spent $600,000 training him. Why would I want somebody to hire his experience?"

Tom Watson's response provides insight to leaders who are tempted to let a staff member go after a mistake or failure. If their mistake was not immoral or fundamentally undermining to the direction of the organization, we might do well to keep them. Why not view it as a learning experience, and consider it an investment in the future?

Failure is the opportunity to
begin again, more intelligently.

—Henry Ford

Once again, Henry Ford's simplicity strikes me. Failure was never final to him, nor was it fatal. Like his contemporary, Thomas Edison, he expected failures on the way to success. It was all part of the learning process. He allowed failure to tutor him, then he continued on down the path that much smarter and wiser.

Show me a thoroughly satisfied man,
and I will show you a failure.

—Thomas Edison

I find it terribly difficult to understand a person who is so satisfied with their present accomplishments that they have no desire to risk attempting something new. There is nothing wrong with spiritual contentment with our possessions and resources, but each of us should carry to our grave a holy dissatisfaction with our achievements.

I will have no man work for me
who has not the capacity
to become a partner.

—J.C. Penney

I have heard many single women say
they won't date a man who isn't a potential
marriage partner. They don't want to waste
their time with unproductive emotional
entanglements. J.C. Penney looked at
employees the same way. He looked for the
raw ability in all of them—the capacity to rise
in the organization. If necessary, it is wise to
create a position for those kind of people
when you find them!

Here lies a man who knew
how to enlist the service
of better men than himself.

—Andrew Carnegie's Tombstone

I am drawn to Carnegie's humility, as well as his talent. He didn't try to do it all or own it all. He once said, "I owe whatever success I have achieved, by the large, to my ability to surround myself with people who are smarter than I am." He knew his own limitations, but that only spurred him on to find associates who didn't have the same ones.

Luck is the residue of design.

—Branch Rickey

People talk a lot about good luck and bad luck. I believe, however, that Branch Rickey was right. Very few outcomes in this cause and effect world are due to chance. Someone has said, "Good luck is what happens when opportunity meets preparation."

All glory comes from
daring to begin.

—Eugene F. Ware

To begin a task is usually the toughest step. Indeed, the journey of a thousand miles begins with a single step, but I've found *that* step keeps most people stationary. The fear of attempting something big immobilizes them. This is why beginning is half the battle, and why all glory comes from daring to begin.

Don't spend a $1.00's worth
of time on a $.10 decision.

I try to invest the appropriate amount of
time and mental energy into every decision I
make. Visualize a scale: on one side is the
weight of how much the decision will cost.
On the other, how much it will benefit.
Balance each decision's potential benefit with
its actual cost.

Nothing gives one person so
much advantage over another
as to remain always cool and
unruffled under all circumstances.

—Thomas Jefferson

Poise comes through maturity. When we get it, and can keep it under pressure, we will have a decided advantage over others. Panicking usually has a negative effect on a situation, but remaining calm and cool enables us to think and act more intelligently. Make it your ambition to never panic.

The moment you stop learning,
you stop leading.

—Rick Warren

Leaders are learners. Once a person feels they have a firm grasp on all the answers, they have quit being teachable and will soon cease from leading. Their thoughts and methods will become dated, and eventually stale. Good leaders are hungry for learning, all the way to the grave.

A person who is successful
has simply formed the habit of
doing things that unsuccessful
people will not do.

Whatever business field you may have chosen, success will follow you if you will consistently do the things and provide the services that others refuse to do and fail to provide. This makes for outstanding leadership and creates a demand for you and what you do.

You can't build a reputation
on what you're going to do.

—Henry Ford

Our reputation is obviously constructed from our track record, not our intentions. As I travel, I meet pastors and businessmen from all over the country. Many of them know the right principles, talk the correct language, and lay the proper plans. Unfortunately, it takes more than that to build a dynamic church or a profitable business. Success is about what we've produced, not what we've planned.

If you want to succeed,
you should strike out on
new paths rather than travel the
worn paths of accepted success.

—John D. Rockefeller Jr.

It's amazing to me that the levels of Olympic competition at the turn of the twentieth century are now the levels at which junior high school students compete. Why is that? During the last one-hundred years, athletes have invariably discovered new ways to run faster, jump higher, and throw farther. Success, therefore, has meant not merely doing what previous champions have done but pioneering new methods.

You cannot push anyone
up the ladder unless he is
willing to climb a little.

—Andrew Carnegie

No one can succeed for you. Success
isn't a gift to be given away. Believe me, I
have tried many times to "jump start" one of
my staff, just to help them make it beyond
where they might have gone alone. Some
responded and rose to the challenge. Others,
despite my optimism, were unable or
unwilling to climb a step up the ladder.

People support what
they help create.

I'm convinced that the surest way to establish a sense of ownership among your constituency is to involve them in the creative process all along the way. You might be able to reach a goal faster on your own, but when you get there you will be just that— on your own. Slow down, and take your people along.

It's what you learn after
you know it all that counts.

—John Wooden

John Wooden has been there. Here's a
coach who could have easily assumed he
knew it all. It's at that point, however, that the
greatest lessons and most profound
discoveries are found. Someone once said:
"We only learn what we already know." When
we get beyond a superficial understanding of
an idea or concept is when the truth really
sinks in.

A good leader is a guy
who can step on your toes
without messing up your shine.

I've seen some of the best pastors and
business executives in the country at work.
They all seem to have the keen ability to
speak the truth, to lay out the imperatives,
and to communicate the marching orders to
their people. At the same time, they do so
with such warmth and understanding, with
such humor and sensitivity that no one feels
pushed. They actually like the experience
and feel they are better for it.

We are what we repeatedly do;
excellence then is not
an act, but a habit.

—Aristotle

Success is not an event. It is an ongoing process we engage in, time and time again. Aristotle says it in a profound way. Anyone can succeed once or twice. And, anyone can fail or lose a battle or two along the way. What we must focus on is the habit of excellence; practicing success, repeatedly, day after day.

Eagles don't flock—you have
to find them one at a time.

—H. Ross Perot

You've probably noticed this too. Unlike most birds, eagles don't fly in flocks. They don't simply fit in. They don't conform to the activities of their own kind. You cannot find them in huge clusters. They are flying alone, ahead of and higher than the other birds. Leaders are like eagles.

A man who has to be
convinced to act before
he acts is not a man of action.

—Georges Clemenceau

I can easily lose patience with people
whom I continually have to persuade before
they will make a move. People of action don't
need a pep talk every time their organization
needs to take a risk. I'm not suggesting we
don't plan, but men of action often embrace
the method that Tom Peters made popular:
"Ready. Fire. Aim."

Be a yardstick of quality.
Some people aren't used
to an environment where
excellence is expected.

—Stephen Jobs

Stephen Jobs, the founder of Apple Computers, understood as well as anyone what it takes to build excellence into people. He knew that most people don't pursue excellence naturally. Pioneering a new corporation, he recognized that he had the opportunity to set a standard from the very beginning. Ultimately, he understood that this could only take place if he became the example of the quality he desired. He had to be the yardstick for excellence.

A man who wants to
lead the orchestra must
turn his back on the crowd.

This little word picture is pregnant with meaning. If a man wants to lead the orchestra, he must first make a solitary decision. He cannot drift along with the crowd, nor can he pay attention to the crowd's response to his leading. He must remain focused, and be willing to stand alone. He must give himself to the few who are cooperating with him, not the masses who are looking on. Finally, even if he yearns for the crowd's applause, that cannot be his goal. His goal must be to lead his orchestra with excellence. The applause is a by-product.

Congealed thinking is
the forerunner of failure ...
make sure you are always
receptive to new ideas.

—George Crane

I don't have to remind you that we live in a world of fast-paced change. We laugh at the fact that the U.S. Patent Office nearly closed down toward the end of the 19th century, because many felt that nothing new could be invented. Those who lead the pack today are those who are not only open to change, but to the new paradigms—whole new ways of looking at established facts. It was the Swiss who invented the digital wristwatch, but because their own watchmakers weren't open to a new idea— the Japanese have capitalized on it ever since.

It's OK to lend a helping hand—
the challenge is getting
people to let go of it.

When something is freely offered for long enough, it is human nature to become dependent upon it. This is the reason behind the cry for welfare reform in our country. People get comfortable with the helping hand, and soon believe they can't live without it. Good leadership empowers people by providing the resources they need to get started, but the goal is to teach them how to be resourceful themselves.

Being in power is like being a lady.
If you have to tell people
you are, you aren't.

—Margaret Thatcher

I love this quote from Margaret Thatcher of England. Any time our leadership is not obvious enough to those around us that it requires an explanation, we're in danger of losing it. If you must continually remind people that you are in control—someone else is likely assuming that role. Leadership should appear natural and be evident to all.

I recommend you to take care
of the minutes, for the hours
will take care of themselves.

—Lord Chesterfield

Sometimes we miss the forest for the trees, and other times we miss the trees for the forest. When we only see the "big picture" and fail to see to it that the "minutes" are dealt with appropriately, we may miss accomplishing our big-picture goals. If we take care of the little things, we can build on that foundation, and eventually the hours will fall into place.

An important question for leaders:
"Am I building people, or building my
dream and using people to do it?"

—John C. Maxwell

Jack Hayford taught me something years ago. He said, "Our goal isn't to build a big church—but, to build big people." If we invest in people and develop them into mission-driven disciples, we will see our dream for the church accomplished. People quickly ascertain whether we are building them or using them.

Learn to say no to the good
so you can say yes to the best.

This is the battleground where I fight
most often. I can easily distinguish between
good and bad. Yet with my disposition, which
wants to do everything, accomplish
everything, and say yes to everything, I need
accountability to choose between good and
best. I have a "hatchet committee" that helps
me say no to the good things along the way.

Outstanding leaders appeal
to the hearts of their followers,
not their minds.

If you reflect on the most well-remembered political leaders in American history, you'll find men who were able to grip the hearts of the people: Lincoln, Roosevelt, Kennedy, Reagan. It's not about partisanship. It's about the ability to cast a vision, to empathize, to spark hope, to speak to the heart. It's not that these leaders didn't use logic; they just traveled beyond logic, to win the hearts of their audience.

No man will make a great leader
who wants to do it all himself, or
to get all the credit for doing it.

— Andrew Carnegie

Leadership, by definition, cannot be a one man show. If I don't possess the humility and desire to enable me to praise others and give them credit for their success, I'll be severely handicapped in my leadership. If my ego is so big that I insist on the applause, attention, and affirmation, potential partners will leave me alone; and I will end up with only what one person can accomplish.

Leadership is not wielding authority—
it's empowering people.

—Becky Brodin

Too many leaders make the mistake of
thinking when they reach the top, it means
they can use their position and power to
force certain behaviors from their
subordinates. We've all made the statement,
"If *I* were in charge—things would be
different. . . ." However, leadership is not
about a power trip, but about giving power to
the people under you. It's about giving them
the tools they need to do the job.

Every great institution is the
lengthened shadow of a single man.
His character determines the
character of his organization.

—Ralph Waldo Emerson

Every organization reflects its leader. There would be no compassionate organization called The Salvation Army if not for William Booth. There would have been no Methodist Awakening if not for John Wesley. The modern missionary movement would not exist without William Carey. God doesn't look for masses, or even for committees, when He wants to do something—He looks for a leader.

The most effective leadership
is by example, not edict.

Nearly 90% of how people learn is visual. It's what they see. Another 9% of our learning is verbal, or what we hear. About 1% is through our other senses. This alone explains why effective leadership is more caught than taught. People need to see a sermon, more than hear it, to really embrace it. A leader's credibility and his right to be followed are based on his life, as much as his lip.

Whistler's Law:
You never know who's right, but
you always know who's in charge.

I've chuckled at the truth of this "law" more than once. There are indeed times when it's difficult to determine who is right. In fact, it may be an issue of subjective opinion in some cases. However, determining who's in charge is not nearly as difficult; just watch the people. When a tough decision needs to be made, who do they look to? Who do they trust? That's the person in charge.

The most pathetic person
in the world is someone who
has sight but has no vision.

—Helen Keller

This is my favorite statement made by Helen Keller, a woman who was blind and deaf all of her life. She said this in response to the question: "What could be worse than being born without any sight?" Vision is non-negotiable for anyone who wants to succeed. It is the blueprint on the inside of a leader, before he ever sees the plan on the outside.

If a man knows not what harbor
he seeks, any wind is the right wind.

—Seneca

This quote from Seneca is indicative of how so many people live their life. Not knowing what long-term direction they are headed for, they bounce around like a ball in a pinball machine. They live reactive lives based on what happens to them rather than pro-active lives based on what values are in them. They live their life "by accident" rather than "on purpose."

It is only as we develop others
that we permanently succeed.

—Harvey S. Firestone

In a word, the goal of a leader is to leave a "legacy." He wants to leave behind something permanent after he dies. He wants to have improved the lives of people in some corner of the world, or better yet, see them engaged in a cause that counts. This doesn't necessarily mean fame or wealth. It simply means people who continue in a mission because he has developed them.

The highest compliment leaders
can receive is the one that is given
by the people who work for them.

To me, success is being respected by those who are closest to me. I want to display integrity to those who see all my warts and wrinkles. I want to have the admiration of my family and my colleagues, the people who see me day in and day out. It's easy to be honored and esteemed by those who are far away and seldom seen. I want to be a hero at home.

It isn't the people you fire
who make our life miserable,
it's the people you don't.

—Harvey Mackay

Throughout my ministry, I've been fascinated by the words Jesus spoke in John 15. Specifically, where He talks about pruning the vine so that the branches could continue to grow. I've met scores of pastors and leaders who are afraid to "prune" when it comes to their staff. They think it would not appear very "Christian." Quite the contrary, the concept is not only biblical, but if we don't practice it in our organizations, someday it may come back to haunt us.

Today a reader—tomorrow a leader.

—W. Fusselman

One of the principles I've always tried to practice is to be well-read. I believe every meeting I enter without the preparation of good information is one where I can't easily assume my leadership role. Knowledge is power. As the leader, I must know more about the options in front of us, than my boards and committees. Reading helps my leading.

The essence of leadership is
a vision you articulate clearly
and forcefully on every occasion.
You can't blow an uncertain trumpet.

—Theodore Hesburgh

I'll never forget hearing the "vision" of the Pepsi company a number of years ago: "The taste of Pepsi-Cola on the lips of everyone in the world." What a huge, overwhelming vision—yet how precise, measurable, and pointed it was. Everyone in the company knew it, and was harnessed to achieve it. Our vision must be heard until our people can embrace it.

Leadership development is
a lifetime journey—not a brief trip.

—John C. Maxwell

I believe this now more than ever.
About fifteen years ago, I thought I had a
handle on leadership. No doubt, I did
understand some significant leadership
principles. But the more I grow, the more I
recognize that my own leadership
development will take a lifetime. It's not
something we can pick up from a weekend
conference. We must commit our lives to it.

The test of leadership:
Turn around and see if
anyone is following you.

This is the acid test of leadership. If you want to evaluate your own leadership, look at the people following you. Is anyone following? What kind of people do you attract? Does your vision compel people to follow? Are they committed to the vision? This is a simple series of questions every leader should ask himself.

If you pay peanuts,
expect to get monkeys.

I believe in having a staff that is "lean and mean" rather than "fat and sassy." As my last church grew, we were able to do so without adding any new staff over a long period of time. The reason? I paid my pastoral staff well, and I got the best. Because I paid them well, I was able to maintain a strong core, and as we grew they assumed multiple responsibilities. And they didn't have to work for peanuts.

It is wonderful when the
people believe in their leader:
but it is more wonderful when
the leader believes in the people!

It is difficult to say which must come first: the leader believing in his people or vice versa. However, I do know this: If a leader begins to believe in his people, it is only a matter of time before both occur. The fundamental step a leader must take is to believe in his people and communicate it to them. Don't ever settle for merely impressing them.

If a leader demonstrates
competency, genuine concern
for others, and admirable
character, people will follow.

—T. Richard Chase

T. Richard Chase distills the basic
components that followers look for in a
leader. Are they competent? Do they really
care for people? Do they possess strong
character? Everything else is icing on the
cake. Followers can endure a wide spectrum
of differences in their leaders, but these three
elements are non-negotiable.

There is no security on this earth—
only opportunity.

I think I first heard this statement as a quote from a general in Word War II. This world we live in does not offer any lasting security. It can't. What it does offer is trials, challenges, and a whole lot of opportunity. Our security can only be found in our obedience to God's call on our lives.

My responsibility is to be
a supervisor, not a super-worker.

—Fred Smith

Sometimes when we experience growth in our organization, we forget that our role as a leader must evolve too. The larger our organization grows, the less we can do by ourselves. We must commit ourselves to the task of oversight, or we will be overworked. While we must always model work, our chief task is empowering others to work.

Vision is the art of
seeing things invisible.

—Jonathan Swift

One of my favorite stories of possessing vision is about Walt Disney. Because Walt had passed away before the Grand Opening of Walt Disney World, Mrs. Disney was asked to appear on the stage at the opening ceremony. When she was introduced to come to the podium and greet the crowd, the master of ceremonies said to her, "Mrs. Disney—I just wish Walt could have seen this!" Mrs. Disney simply responded, "He did!"

Pay now, play later;
play now, pay later.

—John C. Maxwell

I learned this simple truth from my dad. It's helped me to discard the notion of immediate gratification hundreds of times over the years. If I choose to pay the price for my dreams now, I'll enjoy the rewards of those dreams later. However, if I choose to play now, I may not have the opportunity for reward later. I'll be too busy paying the price.

Failure to prepare is preparing to fail.

—Mike Murdock

Oh, I have found this to be true! I want to be prepared for every event I face. That's why I read. That's why I listen to tapes. It's why I study. It's why I dialogue with staff. I want to reduce the "surprise factor" as much as possible—life itself presents enough surprises, even for the thoroughly prepared. When I fail to prepare in one area, I set myself up for potential failure in other areas as well.

A great man is always
willing to be little.

—Ralph Waldo Emerson

Great people have little use for fame
or notoriety; they are consumed with
productivity, not image. They do not feel the
need to project their self-worth to anyone.
They are content when the moment calls for
them to be little, ordinary, or common—as
long as the goal is achieved.

As a rule ... he (or she) who
has the most information will
have the greatest success in life.

—Disraeli

We've all heard it before: knowledge is power. Because there is doubtless truth to this axiom, I consume as much information as I possibly can in a variety of subjects relevant to me and my work. I have noticed that success follows the person who brings something to the table when the meeting begins; they are well-read and well-prepared. They never come across as ignorant in any subject.

Have confidence that if you
have done a little thing well,
you can do a bigger thing well too.

—Storey

Life is full of graduations. In each stage of our journey, God has planned junctions where we will either pass or fail the quiz life has presented. Not only does God promise greater opportunities when we have proven to be faithful in the little things, but we also gain confidence when we've been successful in them. Remember, young David graduated from the bear, to the lion , to the giant.

Dreams are the touchstones
of our character.

—Henry David Thoreau

All across the country, as I meet leaders, one question I enjoy asking them is: "What is your dream?" You can tell a lot about a man's character by the substance and size of his dreams. They speak volumes about his motives, priorities, values, purposes, and goals.

The most important thing
about having goals is have one.

—Geoffrey F. Abert

Simply possessing a goal will put you in a higher league than most of your peers. I remember J. C. Penney once said "Show me a stockclerk with a goal, and I'll show you a man who'll make history. Show me a man without a goal, and I'll show you a stockclerk." Goals make the difference between dreaming and doing.

Some people change jobs, mates,
and friends, but never think of
changing themselves.

We live in a generation consumed with changing exteriors. We've bought into the notion that if we just can change the people, circumstances, and environment around us, we can solve our problems. Most of the time, however, the issue lies within us. God doesn't hold us responsible for what happens to us, but for what happens in us.

If you see a snake, just kill it.
Don't appoint a committee on snakes.

—H. Ross Perot

So much needless red tape exists in many organizations. I hate red tape. I agree with Ross Perot when it comes to the "snakes" of life. If we know what the "bottom line" is, then we can clear any obstacle that prevents that goal. Often, we don't need any further research or discussion; we simply hide behind it because it looks like positive action. Look for ways to realistically solve problems. Activity does not always equal accomplishment.

Lord, when I am wrong, make me
willing to change; when I am right,
make me easy to live with.
So strengthen me that the power
of my example will far exceed
the authority of my rank.

—Pauline H. Peters

What a fitting note to conclude with. This disarming petition forces me, as a leader, to adjust my heart as well as my head. When all is said and done, I want the life I model to speak louder than the degrees, ranks, and titles I may have earned. After all, when my journey is over, I want my leadership to be who I am, not merely what my job description says I do.

About the Author

John Maxwell is one of the world's most respected authorities on leadership and personal effectiveness. He has written more than twenty books, including the *New York Times* best seller *The 21 Irrefutable Laws of Leadership,* which has sold more than half a million copies. In addition to his writing career, he is a popular speaker, inspiring more than 250,000 people annually at appearances nationwide.

Dr. Maxwell's advice is based on his thirty-plus years of experience as a pastoral and organizational leader. He is founder of the INJOY Group, an organization that helps people maximize their personal and leadership potential. And he has served as a senior pastor for churches in California, Ohio, and Indiana.

The father of two grown children, Dr. Maxwell lives in Atlanta, Georgia, with Margaret, his wife of more than twenty-five years.

Additional copies of this book and other titles by John C. Maxwell
are available from your local bookstore.

The Power of Thinking Big
The Power of Influence
The Power of Attitude

RIVER
OAK
PUBLISHING